# THE LAST DAYS OF STEAM
## ON THE SOUTHERN
# SOUTH EASTERN AND CHATHAM

Departing Deepdene with a vigorous display of steam, class U Mogul No. 31611 attacks the 1 in 100 bank to Dorking Town, with a train to Guildford and Reading. The slope of the North Downs is visible beyond, a feature of so many railway lines in Kent and Surrey.

26.5.63

# THE LAST DAYS OF STEAM ON THE SOUTHERN

# SOUTH EASTERN AND CHATHAM

– ALAN POSTLETHWAITE –

ALAN SUTTON PUBLISHING LIMITED

First published in the United Kingdom in 1995 by
Alan Sutton Publishing Ltd · Phoenix Mill · Far Thrupp · Stroud · Gloucestershire

First published in the United States of America in 1995 by
Alan Sutton Publishing Inc. · 83 Washington Street · Dover · NH 03820

British Library Cataloguing in Publication Data

A catalogue record for this book is available from the British Library.

ISBN 0-7509-0826-2

*Endpapers: Front: 'West Country' class Pacific No. 34001* Exeter *stokes up and gathers speed west of Faversham with a Ramsgate to Victoria train. Back: class D1 No. 31489 bursts from beneath an overbridge between Smeeth and Ashford.*

Library of Congress Cataloging in Publication Data applied for

Typeset in 9/10 Palatino.
Typesetting and origination by
Alan Sutton Publishing Limited.
Printed in Great Britain by
Butler & Tanner, Frome, Somerset.

# Introduction

The South Eastern and Chatham Railway (SECR) existed as such for just twenty-four years, until becoming part of the Southern grouping of 1923. Constitutionally, it was not one but two railways:

1. The South Eastern Railway (SER) which took the low road through Tonbridge and Ashford, opening to Folkestone and Dover in 1844.
2. The London, Chatham and Dover Railway (LCDR) which took the high road along the North Downs, opening to Dover in 1862.

During four decades, the two parent companies had competed ruthlessly until merging operationally in 1899. Numerous duplications of lines and services were created, with costly extensions which left both companies virtually bankrupt. At the London end, the LCDR's 'Metropolitan Extensions' to Victoria and Holborn Viaduct were matched by the SER's extension from London Bridge to Cannon Street and Charing Cross. The most prized traffic was to the Channel ports, but the competition spread also to the Isle of Thanet and to most towns between London and the Kent coast.

Proliferation of new lines was not matched by engineering standards of design and construction. This resulted in widespread line restrictions, including axle weight on LCDR bridges and line clearances on the SER, especially south of Tonbridge to Hastings. Although these were progressively eased, it was not until the mid-1980s that all Victorian line restrictions were finally removed.

These line restrictions led to a family of outstanding 4–4–0 express steam engines and to narrow, straight-sided coaching stock, originally with 'birdcage' lookouts for the guards. When Richard Maunsell introduced his first mixed-traffic 2–6–0 (Mogul) in 1917 and his first full-height coaches in 1921, these were regarded as radical departures for the SECR.

Another legacy of early competition was the huge number of route permutations to the Channel coast, especially after the SECR and SR rationalized key junctions and connections. This proved an invaluable asset in times of war and line blockages, but it did not eliminate peak-hour congestion and delays (to London Bridge in particular), caused by the convergence of too many lines.

During the inter-war years, the Southern Railway (SR) electrified the entire SECR suburban network as far as Gillingham, Maidstone, Sevenoaks and Reigate. Steam endured, however, on freight, rural branches and all lines to the coast. As engineering restrictions were eased, more powerful express engines were introduced, including 'King Arthur' and 'Schools' classes, culminating in the Bulleid Pacifics of which forty-eight were named after RAF units from the Battle of Britain.

During the years of BR steam, there remained in service a fine collection of former SECR and SR steam engines, augmented by an influx of 'standard' designs of LMS/BR origin. Great Western engines could also be found on the long SER line from Redhill to Reading. The end of steam came between 1958 and 1965 when electric multiple units (EMUs) and diesels took over, and most of the branch lines were closed.

It is against this unusual background of ancient rivalry and constrained engineering that this book is compiled, with pictures taken between 1958 and 1964, the final flourish of steam. The photographic sequence is a mainline journey from London to Dover, out via Chatham and return via Tonbridge, with excursions along most of the secondary and branch lines en route. We encounter trains, stations, people and lineside accoutrements, in a rich and varied landscape. A total of twenty-three classes of steam engine are recorded, in eight wheel arrangements and with six railways of origin as follows:

| | SER | SECR | SR | GWR | LMSR | BR |
|---|---|---|---|---|---|---|
| 0–6–0 | 01 | C | Q1 | | | |
| 2–6–0 | | N, N1 | U, U1 | | | 4MT |
| 4–4–0 | | D1, E1, L | V | | | |
| 4–6–0 | | | N15 | 78xx | | 4MT, 5MT |
| 4–6–2 | | | MN, WC/BB | | | |
| 0–4–4T | | H | | | | |
| 2–6–2T | | | | | 2MT | |
| 2–6–4T | | | W | | 4MT | 4MT |

The most-photographed engine types are SECR tanks, SECR/SR Moguls and SR Pacifics. Overall, an impression is painted of intense traffic to Thanet and the Channel ports, of busy secondary lines through verdant valleys, and of some delightfully quaint branches which wander through the Weald or over the Thames marshes to the back-of-beyond. A few transitional diesels add a further sparkle of interest to this nostalgic excursion through the 'Garden of England'.

# THE LAST DAYS OF STEAM
## ON THE SOUTHERN
# SOUTH EASTERN AND CHATHAM

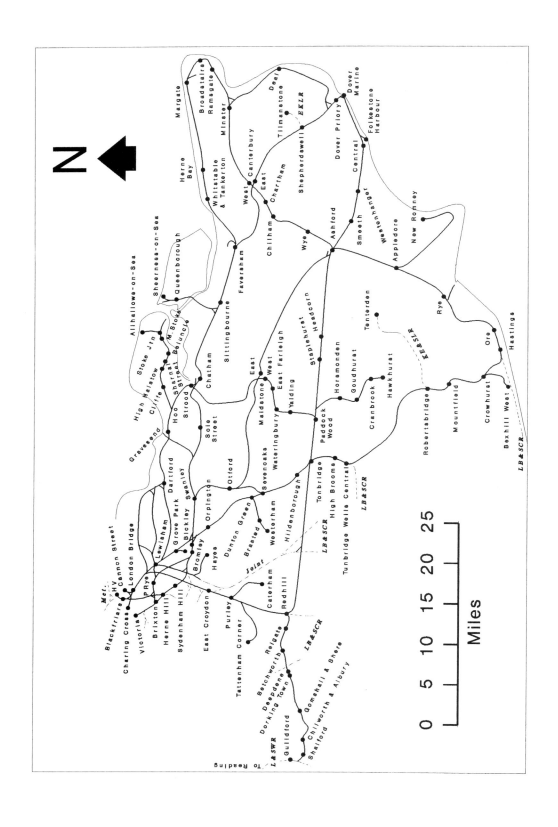

N

Blackfriars
Charing Cross
Cannon Street
London Bridge
Victoria
Met.
HV
Brixton
P Rye
Herne Hill
Sydenham Hill
East Croydon
Purley
Lewisham
Grove Park
Bickley
Bromley
Hayes
Caterham
Tattenham Corner
Dunton Green
Brasted
Westerham
Redhill
Reigate
Betchworth
Deepdene
Dorking Town
Gomshall & Shere
Chilworth & Albury
Shalford
Guildford
L&SWR
To Reading
LB&SCR
Hildenborough
Tunbridge Wells Central
High Brooms
Tonbridge
Paddock Wood
LB&SCR
LB&SCR
Joint
Sevenoaks
Otford
Sole Street
Dartford
Gravesend
Strood
Cliffe
High Halstow
Stoke Jn.
M.Stoke
Sharnal Street
Beluncle
Hoo
Allhallows-on-Sea
Sheerness-on-Sea
Queenborough
Chatham
Sittingbourne
Faversham
Whitstable & Tankerton
Herne Bay
Margate
Broadstairs
Ramsgate
Minster
Deal
Dover Marine
Dover Priory
Folkestone Harbour
EKLR
Tilmanstone
Shepherdswell
Dover Central
West Canterbury
East
Chartham
Chilham
Wye
Ashford
Smeeth
Westenhanger
Appledore
New Romney
Rye
Ore
Hastings
Bexhill West
LB&SCR
Crowhurst
Mountfield
Robertsbridge
Hawkhurst
Cranbrook
Goudhurst
Horsmonden
Tenterden
KE&SLR
Headcorn
Staplehurst
East Farleigh
Yalding
Wateringbury
East West Maldstone
East

0  5  10  15  20  25

Miles

# I – Victoria and Blackfriars to Chatham

Class N Mogul No. 31413 prepares to take empty stock from Victoria to Eardley sidings via Herne Hill, Tulse Hill and Streatham. The shed plate is 73A for Stewarts Lane, a major depot tucked between the viaducts of Battersea. Note the wooden extension to the width of platform 1, part of the Southern's rationalization of the two Victorias in 1923.

27.3.59

The 'Golden Arrow' Pullman service to Paris was inaugurated by the Southern and the Nord in 1929. Platform 8 was its Victoria venue, pictured here with 'Battle of Britain' class Pacific No. 34085 *501 Squadron*, which commemorates the Gravesend-based Hurricanes with ninety-three victories. The large arrow in semi-relief mollifies the 'spam-can' effect of Oliver Bulleid's air-smoothed casing.

7.5.59

Beneath a forest of chimney pots on the 'Chatham' side of Victoria, 'King Arthur' class 4–6–0 No. 30777 *Sir Lamiel* awaits the right of way from platform 1, alongside the ex-SECR signal-box. The backdrop of tall buildings provides a canyon effect, resounding with train noises, similar to Paddington's approaches.

27.3.59

In 1918 Victoria took over from Charing Cross the role of Continental terminus of the SECR. Seething with steam, light Pacific No. 34077 *603 Squadron*, holds a Dover train beneath Ecclestone Bridge in the rather drab setting of platform 2. The engine commemorates the Montrose-based Spitfires which scored ninety-eight victories during the Battle of Britain.

27.3.59

Compared with the Brighton station on the left, Victoria's eastern side was inelegant and somewhat untidy. In platform 8 a fireman fits headcode discs to 'Battle of Britain' class Pacific No. 34087 *145 Squadron*, which commemorates the Hurricane squadron from Westhampnett (Sussex) with fifty-four victories.

9.7.60

The LCDR main line from Victoria opened in 1862, mostly as viaduct as far as Brixton, pictured here with its unusual signal-box, closed a week previously. Class W 2–6–4 tank No. 31912 is en route to Hither Green yard. This powerful class was a derivative of Richard Maunsell's three-cylinder class N1; just five were built between 1931 and 1932 for cross-London freight duties. None is preserved.

14.3.59

'Battle of Britain' class Pacific No. 34088 *213 Squadron* burrows beneath the great span of the LBSCR's South London line at Brixton, with a train for the Channel ports via Tonbridge. It commemorates the Filton-based Hurricanes with eighty-one victories. The bridge is of 'Chatham' design; between Battersea and Loughborough the LCDR built both the South London and its own line.

4.10.59

The parting of ways at the London end of Herne Hill, with rebuilt 'West Country' class Pacific No. 34001 *Exeter* running tender-first to Victoria with empty stock from Eardley sidings. In LCDR days passenger trains would divide here for the City and West End. The line to the right, for Blackfriars, Holborn and Farringdon, has the 'sorting sidings' to either side.

14.5.61

Gantries old and new, with a train of flat trucks coming off the Down sorting sidings at Herne Hill, double-headed by classes N and Q1. The unusual double-point in the foreground leads to the Up sorting sidings where goods trains were marshalled before proceeding to the space-restricted goods station at Blackfriars.

14.3.59

The 'Golden Arrow' was the SR's most prestigious boat train and a brilliant piece of public relations. Sir John Elliot initiated the Southern's good PR, later becoming SR General Manager, then Chairman of the Railway Executive and of London Transport. With flags-a-fluttering, the Down 'GA' approaches Herne Hill, headed by unrebuilt 'West Country' class Pacific No. 34092 *City of Wells*.

4.10.59

With a fine display of smoke and power, class N Mogul No. 31410 and an illegible class Q1 0–6–0 approach Herne Hill's platform 4 with a freight from the sorting sidings. At the end of the Up island platform, redundant gantries of LCDR lattice type have lost their signal arms and await demolition.

14.3.59

Six months later, at the London end of Herne Hill, all lattice gantries have gone except for these elevated shunting signals, partly obscured by a crude electric lamp. Passing at speed with a Channel boat train is 'Battle of Britain' class Pacific No. 34089 *602 Squadron*, commemorating the Glasgow-based Spitfires with 102 victories.

13.9.59

Penge tunnel, a mile and a quarter long, is bored through London clay and is lined with bricks baked from its own spoil. Because of smoke obscuration within the tunnel, repeater distant signals were provided, one of which is seen here at the Sydenham Hill end. The light engine is D1 4–4–0 No. 31749, an express class once the pride of the SECR.

4.4.59

'Schools' class V No. 30938 *St Olave's* speeds past Dulwich College estates, on the approach to Sydenham Hill, with a train to Ramsgate. The Saxby & Farmer signal-box is of a type also found on the LBSCR and other railways. Note too the LCDR finials and lattice signal posts. *St Olave's* was the only grammar school in class V, possibly held in particular esteem by the SR management because of its proximity to London Bridge station. The school has since moved to Orpington.

4.4.59

Looking north from the closed Ludgate Hill station: to the right is Holborn Viaduct terminus with its triple roof; the lines under the signal-box descend steeply through Snow Hill to Farringdon, where the LCDR made important links with the Metropolitan, Midland and Great Northern railways. Through passenger services ceased in 1916 and freight ended in 1969. Through passenger services to the Midlands were revived in 1988 (as Thameslink) when Holborn Viaduct was closed.

7.3.59

The north end of the original Blackfriars station, on the south bank of the Thames, was used as a terminus from 1864 until the bridge opened in 1865. The lines pass over Alexandra Bridge to the (new) Blackfriars–Ludgate Hill–Holborn complex of stations. Note the similarity of the bridge design to that of Brixton. Note also the courses of light brickwork in the tower, a characteristic of many LCDR structures.

7.3.59

The original Blackfriars subsequently became Southwark goods station. Here, at the south end of the old shed, class E1 No. 31507 awaits duty on an RCTS special from Liverpool Street to Gravesend West Street: out via Canonbury, East Finchley, King's Cross, Snow Hill, Crayford and Chislehurst; back via the East London line. In 1921 Maunsell rebuilt a batch of Wainwright class E with a larger superheated boiler; they were designated class E1 and were very similar to class D1.

21.3.59

The high-level sidings at Blackfriars were mostly to the east of the running lines, with wagon hoists (seen here) to the low-level for loading and unloading. Because of limited shunting space, goods trains were pre- and post-sorted at the Herne Hill sorting sidings. The LNER coaches on this train belong to the RCTS 'London and North Kent' railtour.

21.3.59

On the 'Chatham' side of Peckham Rye, a freight from Hither Green yard is headed by class C 0–6–0 No. 31317. The wooden platforms and heavy awning are of LBSCR design – the two lines between Loughborough and Peckham were both constructed by the LBSCR, opening in 1865–6. The LCDR line originally ran to Crystal Palace high-level to serve the Great Exhibition; the Greenwich Park branch was added in 1871–88, followed by the Catford Loop in 1892.

2.4.60

About 25 ft tall and beautifully cast is the LCDR insignia on the south abutment of Alexandra Bridge, together with the faded 'Southern Railway' painted on the stonework. The wagon-turntable once served the modest wharf, part of Southwark low-level goods station. Although the bridge and wharf are now demolished, the casting has been restored in striking colours for all to admire from Blackfriars road bridge.

28.5.60

At the former Lewisham Road station, 'West Country' class Pacific No. 34025 *Whimple* approaches Parks Bridge with a Victoria to Ramsgate train, diverted via the Dartford Loop. This was once the Greenwich Park branch which closed in 1917. The Lewisham spur opened in 1929 to relieve London Bridge of commuter and freight traffic. Parks Bridge collapsed in 1957 when a steam train on the SER main line below ran into an EMU, causing ninety fatalities, the Southern's greatest tragedy.

26.4.59

Bromley South was a popular pick-up point for steam excursions to the Kent coast. A grimy 4–6–0, BR class 4 No. 75066, arrives in platform 4 with a train for Chatham and Dover. The line from here to St Mary Cray opened in 1858 as the Mid-Kent Railway, taken over by the LCDR in 1863. The original route into Victoria ran via Crystal Palace (low-level) and Clapham Junction, until the LCDR opened its own main line via Herne Hill in 1863.

14.6.59

At Bickley Junction these SECR signal gantries with co-acting arms cry out to be seen from afar. A class U1 Mogul heads a Victoria train from Dover, Ashford and Maidstone East. Civil work is in progress, part of the modernization to ease curves between the LCDR and SER main lines, and to quadruple the tracks from here to Swanley. The gantries and finials date from the 1914 rationalization of the junction, which created numerous new route permutations to the coast.

30.8.58

The evening sun picks up reflected trackwork and exhaust steam from a class N Mogul as it climbs the five miles of Sole Street bank at 1 in 100. The LCDR followed the North Downs from near Swanley to Dover, necessitating steep grades and tunnels, together with bridges and viaducts across the valleys of the Cray, Darent, Medway and Stour. The LCDR route distance to Dover Marine was 78 miles from Victoria, compared with the SER's 77 miles from Charing Cross (via Sevenoaks).

14.6.59

An unidentified 'Schools' approaching Swanley brings a train off the LCDR main line from Chatham. To its left the Sevenoaks/Maidstone East line passes a 4-SUB unit in the siding. On the far side work is in progress for impending colour-light signalling and changes of track designation from U-U-D-D to U-D-U-D, so reverting to the pre-1939 arrangement of the original junction station which was located just to the right of this picture.

21.4.59

Having just crossed the Medway, a standard class 4 locomotive coasts towards Rochester with a train to Dover. A challenge to modellers, lineside features (right to left) include: Rochester Town Hall; the Gaumont cinema; the old signal-box and its replacement power box (rarely modelled together); and the goods yard, site of the former SER station, Rochester Common. The line tunnels through the next hill to emerge at Chatham. Charles Dickens decried the loss of playing fields here due to railway construction.

14.6.59

As the dominant name of both the LCDR and the SECR, one somehow expected grandeur at Chatham rather than these simple platforms wedged between tunnel portals in the chalk. Class N Mogul No. 31412 is seen arriving with a Victoria to Ramsgate train of Maunsell stock. This was the first section of the East Kent Railway (the original name of the LCDR), opening from Faversham to Strood in 1858, with running powers over the SER's North Kent line to London Bridge. The SER should have absorbed this up-start, but chose instead to oppose and hinder.

26.3.59

In Chatham station, standard 4–6–0 No. 75066 awaits the green light with a train to Dover. Chatham tunnel is just discernible through the murk, beyond the tall overbridge. The pile of debris, broken platform surface, cast-iron bracket, gas lamp and general gloom evoke an atmosphere of antiquity, but the EMU stop-signs, tall BR tender and new colour-light signals betray the fact that Chatham was in its last days of steam.

14.6.59

# II – Branches to Allhallows and Sheerness

Class H tank No. 31263 awaits departure to Allhallows-on-Sea with a van, coach and push-pull set. This was the last pocket of steam in North Kent, looking somewhat incongruous on Gravesend Central's electrified tracks. The SER's North Kent line to Strood was opened in 1845–7; it was electrified to Gravesend in 1930 and to Gillingham and Maidstone West in 1939, carrying mainly commuter traffic.

1.8.60

During the late 1950s coaches from all three pre-Group companies could be found on the Allhallows branch. Tucked into the bay between Gravesend's Down platform and the goods shed is push-pull set No. 481, comprising the coach sections of two ex-SECR railmotors. The LSWR coach roof on the left belongs to set No. 737.

14.12.58

Push-pull set No. 737 of ex-LSWR corridor stock is propelled into Gravesend Central by class H tank No. 31512, in readiness for a trip to Allhallows. Ashing and coaling were carried out in the Down yard, while water was taken between the two Up roads from the column seen here on the left.

14.12.58

Below a fine piece of school architecture, class H tank No. 31263 stands in the service siding on Gravesend's Down side. A shovel-load of fine coal hurtles through the air, apparently directed from the steel mineral wagon. Today this engine is restored on the Bluebell line in Sussex.

1.8.60

Gravesend Central is approached from either direction under a succession of road bridges. Class H tank No. 31193 is seen here with an Allhallows train, gathering speed on the town's eastern fringes; note the old habit of keeping curtains three-quarters closed during the daytime. Notice also the twin chimneys of Bowaters paper mill which once connected with the LCDR at Gravesend West Street.

1.8.60

While there were simple 'occupational halts' at Denton, Hoo junction and Uralite, the first real station on the Allhallows branch was here at Cliffe. Ready to depart with an Up train, class H tank No. 31512 stands alongside a fine arc-roof canopy, a characteristic of many SER stations, for example Ashford. The style of building – weather-boarded and single-storey – could also be found elsewhere on the SER, for example Deepdene and Westerham.

14.12.58

Between High Halstow and Sharnal Street, push-pull set No. 737 is propelled by class H tank No. 31512. The up-sun aspect brings out the relief and detail of the coach-sides as well as the strong, square silhouette of the SR signal. The ex-LSWR stock comprises a corridor-composite and a brake-third.

14.12.58

Class H tank No. 31193 brings a Maunsell set through a shallow cutting just west of High Halstow halt. It seems incongruous that prestige boat trains from Charing Cross once graced this humble line to Port Victoria. Paddle-steamers would then cross to the LCDR's Queenborough Pier (Isle of Sheppey) to connect with Continental ferries to Flushing. It was an example of wildest inter-company rivalry.

1.8.60

A crystal-clear shot of an Up train headed by class H tank No. 31193 between High Halstow and Cliffe, near the village of Cooling. This is Dickensian country, the opening landscape of *Great Expectations*, which can scarcely have changed but for the coming of the railway.

1.8.60

The western end of the Hoo peninsula had some idyllic settings for depicting country branch trains. Here, class H tank No. 31263 hauls a couple of old coaches past High Halstow's Down fixed distant. The Hundred of Hoo branch opened in 1882 to Port Victoria, 12½ miles from Hoo junction. The sub-branch to Allhallows was built much later by the SR.

1.8.60

Most of the Hoo peninsula is bleak, marshy and exposed to the east wind, but there are orchards in the more sheltered south-west. Near the village of Hoo, a cherry tree frames a brace of push-pull sets, bound for Gravesend. All three pre-Group companies are represented: SECR tank No. 31263, LSWR coaches at the front and LBSCR at the rear.

1.8.60

With a full head of steam and cylinder drains open, class H tanks Nos 31263 and 31193 draw away from the neat and elegant Sharnal Street station. The engines and stock have been doubled to cater for the Bank Holiday traffic. There were sidings here to connect with the Chattenden Naval Tramway which carried explosives, and with the Kingsnorth Light Railway which served former airship sheds on the Medway.

1.8.60

Beluncle halt was opened in 1906, comprising just a short platform. Miskin siding(s) would appear to pre-date the halt, hence the different name. The scene is enhanced by the strong sunlight and storm-clouds.

1.8.60

Cloud and sky colour provide modest relief in the wilderness of the Hoo peninsula, sufficient to make an ordinary train interesting. Near Middle Stoke halt, with the Medway salt marshes on the left, this Down train is headed by class H tank No. 31263.

1.8.60

Silent sentinel of the marshes, an SR signal with rail-built post beckons a train of oil tankers, headed by class Q1 0–6–0 No. 33032. British Petroleum's Isle of Grain oil refinery is on the horizon, near the former terminus of Port Victoria. But for this refinery, opened in 1951, the Hundred of Hoo line would probably have closed completely under the Beeching axe.

4.2.60

A colourful train of oil tankers, headed by class Q1 No. 33032, approaches Stoke Junction halt. The five-plank wagons provide a suitable distance to minimize fire risk from exhaust sparks.

4.2.60

A push-pull set of ex-LSWR stock departs Stoke junction, headed by class H tank No. 31553. The Down signals are respectively for Allhallows and Grain. Medway ferry services ceased in 1897 when Port Victoria's pier was wrecked in a gale. The pier was reopened from 1900 to 1904 for Continental ferries, following a fire on Sheppey's Queenborough Pier. Neither 'port' was substantial.

4.2.60

On a bleak winter's day, across the windswept marshes between the Medway and the Thames, the silhouette of a class H tank propels its tiny train towards Allhallows-on-Sea, with the Isle of Grain oil refinery breaking the monotony of the leaden horizon.

4.2.60

The sub-branch to Allhallows-on-Sea was just under two miles long and opened in 1932. SR in character, its assets included this unusual baked-bean can of a water tower, set upon a single massive girder. Trains were predominantly pre-Group, as seen here with LSWR coaches and SECR tank. The gallant photographer, who may have been a local man, is sporting a flash camera, bicycle clips and what appears to be a railway cap.

4.2.60

The station at Allhallows comprised an island platform with run-round loops, plus a few sidings and a turntable. It was designed for much longer trains than this push-pull set, part of a grand plan for commuting and holiday traffic which never materialized. Used mainly for day excursions, Allhallows-on-Sea was one of London's closest but least attractive resorts, regarded by many during its latter years as 'the end of the line' (in all senses).

4.2.60

The full splendour of Allhallows-on-Sea, with a row of caravans by the sea-shore. Note the turntable in the field, and the shadow of the gantry with its generous array of four Home signals. When first opened, the sub-branch was so well patronized that it was soon doubled to Stoke Junction. It closed in 1961.

4.2.60

Just across the Medway, the Isle of Sheppey has a topography similar to the bleak end of the Hoo peninsula. This is Sheerness-on-Sea, a former Royal Dockyard town served by a branch of the LCDR. The engine is ex-SECR class C No. 31495 and the coach on the left is ex-LSWR. Surprisingly for mid-June, these ladies are wearing topcoats as they return from a morning shopping trip to Sittingbourne.

14.6.59

A 'concerto in C' as Wainwright 0–6–0 No. 31495 runs round its train at Sheerness. Exhaust-beat and wheel-squeal would soon be music of the past, for this is the last day of steam on the branch. It survived the Beeching inquisition to serve a thriving town and resort, so much larger than neighbouring Allhallows.

14.6.59

Shaded by the roof of the closed signal-box, an up-sun shot of an Ivatt class 2 (ex-LMS) 2–6–2T bringing a train into Sheerness-on-Sea. The branch was nine miles long. At Queenborough it once junctioned with the Sheppey Light Railway and with the spur to Queenborough Pier. The latter closed in 1923 when its ferry service to Flushing was transferred to Folkestone.

14.6.59

New flat-bottom track has been laid at Sheerness-on-Sea, with a platform now long enough for twelve-coach EMUs from London. Class C No. 31495 has just added a set of BR 'blood-and-custard' Mark 1s to the Maunsell set. This terminus opened in 1883 as the town expanded eastwards. Until a direct loop was added in 1922, trains ran via the original 1860 terminus at Sheerness Dockyard. The latter survived as a goods station until 1963.

14.6.59

The window of a Maunsell straight-sided coach is put to reflective use on the Sheerness branch, with class C No. 31495 heading a train on the curve out of Sittingbourne. A second spur served the branch from the London direction.

14.6.59

After arrival and uncoupling at Sittingbourne, 0–6–0 class C No. 31495 takes water before running round its train for the return to Sheerness-on-Sea. The composition is unusually stark and uneasy, and one is somehow reminded of the Elvis Presley hit of that era, *Love Me Tender*.

14.6.59

The last days of steam were also the last of many local goods yards and sheds which provided points of interest for the traveller. The brick shed, associated huts and open truck enhance this scene at Sittingbourne, balanced by the class C locomotive on the branch platform. The centre-piece is BR class 4MT 4–6–0 No. 75066, ready to depart with a train to Dover.

14.6.59

Class N features are brought out in this shot of No. 31402 arriving at Sittingbourne with a train for Ramsgate. Richard Maunsell did not design his Mogul for good looks, but as a utilitarian First World War workhorse for mixed-traffic duty. The protruding deflector plates, narrow waist, prominent rodding and piping made them ungainly, almost French-American in style. They were more graceful before the deflector plates were added.

14.6.59

# III – Faversham to Thanet and Dover

Class N Mogul No. 31824 cuts through grasses and wild flowers near Faversham, with a 'fitted', Continental mixed bag of vans from Bricklayer's Arms, running via Chislehurst and Chatham to Dover.
14.6.59

'Schools' class V No. 30919 *Harrow* arrives at Faversham with a Victoria to Dover train. Note the valancing to the platform canopies, a simple pattern found throughout the LCDR.
14.6.59

First of its class, rebuilt 'West Country' class Pacific No. 34001 *Exeter* stokes up and gathers speed west of Faversham with a Ramsgate to Victoria train. The very trees seem to yield in the presence of this monster of steam.

14.6.59

A hundred numbers on and still wearing its air-smoothed casing, SR Pacific No. 34101 *Hartland* drifts through a wooded cutting near Faversham with a boat train to Victoria; a steam swansong indeed, for this was the last day of steam on the LCDR main line. The third rail is laid and the semaphore signals are already dismantled.

14.6.59

Class D1 4–4–0 No. 31494, almost brushes the foliage with a parcels/baggage train from Dover to Victoria, a mile or two west of Faversham. The driver, who is keeping a keen eye on proceedings, is putting his sight at risk; unlike their French counterparts, British enginemen seldom wore goggles.

14.6.59

Following close behind the 'parcels' in the previous picture, a track-level shot of class N Mogul No. 31411 with a passenger train from Dover. These might well have been two halves of the same boat train, noble duty indeed for the mundane N. Comparison of these pictures shows clear design similarities between classes D1 and N.

14.6.59

BR class 4 No. 75066 pauses at Faversham with a train for Ramsgate, with the focus of attention upon the fireman and guard. The picture also brings out the high running plate which gave excellent access for maintenance of the cylinders, mechanisms and wheels.

14.6.59

At Faversham's country end, colour-light signals are about to replace this fine array of semaphore starters and their LCDR lattice posts and finials. 'West Country' class Pacific No. 34025 *Whimple* will shortly bear left past the engine shed to the Isle of Thanet. This engine, water crane, brazier and elderly crew would not see another winter of service here.

26.4.59

'King Arthur' class N15 No. 30800 *Sir Meleaus de Lile* arrives at Faversham with a train from Ramsgate to Victoria. This was a wonderful station for parades of historic engines and rolling stock, here in their last days of Kent coast service.

14.6.59

Apparently crewless, an ex-SECR class C No. 31714 is on shunting duty with an ex-SR brake van, by the Shepherd Neame brewery on the north side of Faversham station. Faversham was a major centre of LCDR agricultural traffic, equivalent to the SER's Paddock Wood. The sidings here also served the spur to Faversham Quay, just to the north of the town, which closed during the 1960s.

26.4.59

The mass of pointwork and sidings at the eastern end of Faversham greets the arrival of 'Schools' class 4–4–0 No. 30921 *Shrewsbury* with a train from Ramsgate. Old and new (signal-boxes and rolling stock) are a reminder that this was the last day of regular steam in north-east Kent.

14.6.59

Looking back at Faversham from the Dover line, amid much litter on the track, an Ivatt class 2 tank prepares to move a train from a carriage-cleaning siding. The new power signal-box is ready but not fully in commission.

29.3.59

A train of pure Maunsell composition, curving on to the Isle of Thanet line, is flanked by Faversham's engine shed and goods yard. Class N Mogul was introduced by the SECR in 1917, and a total of eighty were built. No. 31861, seen here, is a 'Woolworth', from a batch of fifty whose parts were manufactured at Woolwich Arsenal between 1924 and 1925, to alleviate redundancy of the former munitions workers.

14.6.59

Light Pacific No. 34068 *Kenley* passes though Whitstable and Tankerton with an immaculate train for the Kent coast. The train must have been a special for it includes several Pullman coaches not generally seen on this line since discontinuation of the 'Thanet Belle' in 1958. The engine commemorates the Surrey aerodrome which controlled Sector 17 during the Battle of Britain.

26.4.59

No. 34025 *Whimple* was one of the more obscure locations of the 'West Country' class Pacifics; until 1948 its name was *Rough Tor*. Here it awaits the green flag in Whitstable's Down platform. Another railway obscurity was the Canterbury and Whitstable line which crossed the far bridge in this picture. Built in 1830 to connect with sailing barges and coasters, the C&W was southern England's first passenger railway. It closed to passengers in 1931 and to all traffic in 1952.

26.4.59

An unidentified class N Mogul, maid of all duties, pauses at Herne Bay with an Up passenger train. This line originated as the Herne Bay & Faversham Railway, changing its name to the Margate & London, then to the Kent Coast Railway, reaching Ramsgate in 1863. It was worked from the outset by the LCDR who purchased it in 1871. Long-distance commuting traffic developed along this coast during SR days, mostly terminating at Cannon Street.

26.4.59

The fine lines of Richard Maunsell's 'Schools' class V, represented here by No. 30935 *Sevenoaks*, at rest at Margate. Introduced in 1930 to replace SECR class L, they were used mainly to Thanet and Hastings, and in latter years to the south-west. From the front there is a family resemblance to the 'King Arthur' 4–6–0s (p. 43 top). In performance, they were the equal of their elder, big cousins.

26.4.59

From three-quarters rear, the 'Schools' class had a fine, angular 'modern' appearance. No. 30935 *Sevenoaks* is seen here at the western end of Margate. This ex-LCDR station was rebuilt by the SR in 1926 and handled vast amounts of excursion traffic from the Midlands and south-east London. The beach is just a few hundred yards beyond Rice & Son. The SER terminus, Margate Sands, was even nearer the sea, but entailed a longer route from London via Tonbridge, Ashford and Ramsgate.

26.4.59

In 1921 the SECR departed from its 'birdcage' coach philosophy to build the 'Continental' stock – tall and narrow with inward-opening doors. There were corridor connections between coaches, except at the guard's end which had rear windows but no forward look-out. This is 'the end of the line' for Second Brake No. 3589, built in 1924–5. Soon to be dismembered, special Set 696 is in store on a long siding near Margate, part of the old SER line from Ramsgate which closed in 1926. The coach end also reveals former Set No. 900.

26.4.59

An ex-SECR 'birdcage' brake-third finds a new lease of life at East Croydon, shown here for comparison with the 'Continental' brake in the previous picture. (Birdcage stock had by now disappeared from regular service.) Although this example is modified and neglected, with door-handles missing, its fine panelling and Edwardian elegance can still be appreciated.

11.5.63

In store near Margate (part of Set 696), is the plush, sumptuous interior of an Open Second coach of 1931 vintage. This was originally a General Saloon or 'Nondescript', comprising three saloons which could be designated 1st, 2nd or 3rd class according to traffic needs. Used on boat trains for Dover, Folkestone and Gravesend, they provided Britain's last 2nd class services (for passengers holding 2nd class ferry tickets). They were later redesignated Open Seconds (equivalent to the old 3rd class) – marvellous value for money!

26.4.59

A study of an SR rail-built signal and yard lamp at Broadstairs, with an evening train departing for Victoria headed by BR standard class 5 No. 73082. The crimson and cream coaches are BR Mark 1s. This was originally the first station out of Ramsgate Harbour, the former LCDR terminus on the beach which closed in 1926 and became a fairground.

26.4.59

In the 1926 rationalization of Thanet, the SR built a new through-station at Ramsgate, a mile from the sea, plus a new loop between the former SER and LCDR lines. This scene across allotments shows part of the new loop. The steam train, headed by a Mogul, has just departed Ramsgate in the Broadstairs direction. The Hastings DMU was making a rare visit to Thanet.

26.4.59

This is a small tribute to the East Kent Light Railways which served the Kent coalfield, one of Colonel Stephens' little lines. Opened in 1912, it remained independent until railway Nationalization in 1948. This is Tilmanstone, the last Kent colliery to survive, and the last resting place for an ex-Great Central five-plank truck – which might easily be mistaken for a Peco Wonderful Wagon under construction.

23.3.61

A study of *Sir Dodinas le Savage*, alias 'King Arthur' class N15 No. 30796, which is about to depart Canterbury East with a train for Dover. Originally introduced by the LSWR in 1918 to the design of Urie, the SR improved the design under Maunsell. To name them after characters from Arthurian legend was a PR inspiration which won favour with the public, making this a much-loved class.

29.3.59

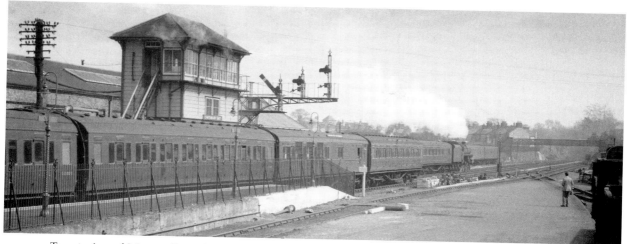

Two trains of Maunsell stock pass at Canterbury East, with an unidentified BR standard 4–6–0 departing for Dover. Dominating the scene is the stilted signal-box which was unique on the LCDR.

29.3.59

Against a stormy sky, the plume of 'King Arthur' class N15 No. 30769 *Sir Balan* is displayed at Canterbury East, and the right of way towards Faversham is set by the neat SR rail-built signal. The engine was from a batch of twenty-nine introduced in 1925 with low cab-roofs to suit restricted clearances on the ex-SECR system.

29.3.59

Railway pictures in the rain are rare. Here at Canterbury East, puddles reflect the stilted signal-box while rainwater gushes from the tender and coach gutters as class Q1 0–6–0 No. 33037 grinds to a halt with a stopping train to Dover. An EMU lurks menacingly in the background, waiting to take over the franchise, but electrification programmes have apparently ignored the ancient gas lamps on the platform.

29.3.59

Dover Priory was rebuilt by the Southern in 1932, incorporating steel canopies and an enclosed footbridge. Witnessed by a lone passenger, class Q1 No. 33037 latches on to the rear of an arrival from Ashford. Beyond, Dover Harbour tunnel leads to the docks and Marine station.

29.3.59

Pride of the Bulleid fleet and first of its class, 'Merchant Navy' class Pacific No. 35001 *Channel Packet* accelerates through Dover Priory with a boat train to Victoria. In the other platform Fairburn class 4 tank No. 42076 stands with a local train.

29.3.59

A touch of the LMS, as Fairburn 2–6–4 tank No. 42076 arrives at Dover Priory with a train from Ashford via Minster and Deal. Like Chatham, this station was sandwiched between tunnel portals in the North Downs. The signal-box is of 1930 vintage.

29.3.59

After tunnelling through the White Cliffs, the LCDR emerges abruptly on to reclaimed land by Dover's western docks. 'West Country' class Pacific No. 34014 *Budleigh Salterton* emerges here with the Up 'The Man of Kent', an impressive title for a train which meandered between Margate and Charing Cross via Ramsgate, Deal, Folkestone and Tonbridge. Inaugurated by BR in 1953, the name endured until the end of steam.

29.3.59

An extra crewman hitches a ride in the spacious cab of 'King Arthur' class N15 No. 30800 *Sir Meleaus de Lile* running tender-first towards Dover Marine. This engine was from a batch of thirteen introduced in 1926, originally with six-wheel tenders to suit the short turntables of the LBSCR. The buildings on the Western Heights are part of Dover Barracks.

29.3.59

Headed by an unidentified Mogul, the Kent portion of the weekday through-working from Birkenhead (via Wolverhampton, Oxford, Reading and Redhill) passes Dover's western docks en route to Sandwich. This is the site of the LCDR's Town & Harbour station, which opened in 1861 and closed in 1927.

29.3.59

A train of Maunsell stock and an unidentified class N pass Dover's western docks before branching right at Hawkesbury Street junction towards Folkestone. The line to the left leads to Marine station and the 'Night Ferry' dock. The roof just to the right of the cranes belongs to the former Lord Warden Hotel, that 'stationary edifice' described by Charles Dickens when awaiting the arrival of the night packet.

29.3.59

SS *Shepperton Ferry* was one of the Southern's coal-fired train ferries commissioned in 1936 for the Dover–Dunkirk service. It could accommodate 12 sleeping cars and some 40 goods wagons or up to 100 motor cars. It is moored here at the seaward end of Admiralty Pier, beyond Dover Marine station. In *The Uncommercial Traveller*, Dickens portrays less comfortable accommodation on the open deck of a paddlesteamer, arriving in Calais cold, wet and salted after a rough crossing.

29.3.59

In 1928 the SR built a new MPD on Dover's beach by the SER main line. Arriving with a boat train is 'Merchant Navy' class Pacific No. 35028 *Clan Line*. On shed are a light Pacific and class O1 No. 31425, a remnant of Victorian design with springs above the tender footplate. This 0–6–0 was built by the SER in 1897 to the design of James Stirling, and was later rebuilt by the SECR with a domed boiler and improved cab. Its duties here were East Kent coal traffic and docks piloting.

29.3.59

Departing Dover on to the SER main line, simply seething with steam, is 'West Country' class Pacific No. 34092 *City of Wells*. The massive footbridge leads to Marine station whose stonework is discernible. This SECR terminus was opened to military traffic in 1914 and to the public in 1919. Renamed Dover Western Docks in its latter years, it was closed in 1994, having been eclipsed by Eurostar and the Channel Tunnel.

29.3.59

The Up 'Golden Arrow' steams beneath the chalk of Shakespeare Cliff, half a mile out of Dover on the SER main line. It is headed by rebuilt 'Merchant Navy' class Pacific No. 35015 *Rotterdam Lloyd*. The 'GA' achieved shorter journey times than other boat trains because customs delays were minimal; heavy luggage was inspected *in absentia* and delivered later to passengers' addresses in London or Paris.

29.3.59

Departing Dover Marine past the engine shed is 'Battle of Britain' class Pacific No. 34071 *601 Squadron*, commemorating the Tangmere-based Hurricanes with seventy-three victories. This is Archcliffe junction, with the Hawkesbury Street curve from the LCDR coming in from the right. The picture is taken from the one surviving platform of the SER's Dover Town station, which opened in 1844 and closed in 1914.

29.3.59

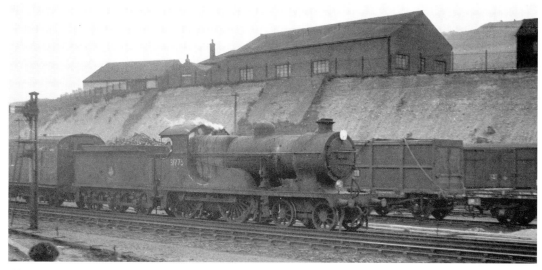

Class L 4–4–0 No. 31775 heads a Margate train on Dover's Hawkesbury Street curve. Although the engine is filthy and the picture is aesthetically unremarkable, it is historically interesting. Designed for express passenger duty under the direction of Wainwright, with improvements by Maunsell, a total of twenty-two were built in 1914 (see also p. 76 top). None is preserved.

29.3.59

# IV – Folkestone and Canterbury to Ashford

The SER signal-box at Folkestone Central, slowly being engulfed by a new platform canopy. A mixed goods train stands in the Down platform, while Bo-Bo type 2 diesel-electric locomotive No. D5005 arrives with a train to Ashford. Fifteen of these 1,160 hp diesels were on loan from LM Region until delivery of the Southern's own 1,550 hp type 3. Introduced prior to electrification to take over freight, they were also tried on passenger duties.

23.3.61

Of the 110 light Pacifics built by the Southern, sixty were rebuilt by BR, losing their air-smoothed casing in the process. Opinion is divided as to whether this improved or detracted from their appearance. Photographed near Smeeth, this rebuilt 'West Country' No. 34100 *Appledore* looks a splendid sight at the head of the Up 'Golden Arrow'.

23.3.61

By contrast, unrebuilt Pacific No. 34083 *605 Squadron* looks drab as it passes through Smeeth station (closed to passengers in 1954) with an Up parcels. The comparison is not entirely valid, however, since this engine is unclean and does not carry the attractive insignia of the 'GA'. Its name commemorates the Turnhouse-based Hurricane crews from Scotland with fifty-six victories during the Battle of Britain.

23.3.61

Near Smeeth, Maunsell class U1 Mogul No. 31908 heads a Continental fitted-freight, including two wagon-loads of motor-car exports. The clean locomotive and crisp plume make this an attractive picture, every rivet showing on the front beam. No. 908 is from a batch of twenty built at Eastleigh in 1931. None is preserved. Their prototype was a rebuild of the only three-cylinder version of class K tank, No. 890 *River Frome*.

23.3.61

Issuing great clouds of exhaust steam, class D1 No. 31489 bursts from beneath an overbridge between Smeeth and Ashford. Class D was Wainwright's first 4–4–0 express class of which fifty-one were built between 1901 and 1903. No. 489 was from the final batch of ten, built for the SECR by Dubs and Co. From 1921 many were rebuilt and superheated by Maunsell as class D1, performing brilliantly. Just one is preserved – No. 737 – in the National Collection at York.

23.3.61

Mounted regally like a cathedral organ, the elevated signal-box at Canterbury West is shrouded in the exhaust of 'Schools' class V No. 30935 *Sevenoaks* as it departs with a train to Ramsgate. At this spot the Canterbury and Whitstable Railway once crossed the SER on the level. Not until taken over by the SER in 1853 was a junction made for C&W trains to enter the SER station.

24.3.61

The spacious, neatly designed layout of Canterbury West, with Bo-Bo type 2 diesel-electric locomotive No. D5014 departing for Ashford with a set of Maunsells and three vans. In the departure platform beyond, Bulleid class Q1 No. 33015 stands with a goods train. This was a curious choice of duties, since such diesels were introduced specifically for freight.

24.3.61

In the Stour Valley south of Canterbury, class N Mogul No. 31403 heads a short train of Mark 1 coaches, bound for Ashford. The graceful road bridge carries the A28. The LCDR main line to Faversham runs parallel to the SER along this stretch, half a mile to the left, further elevated by some 70 ft, and climbing.

24.3.61

Class N1 Mogul was a three-cylinder derivative of the ubiquitous class N, but somewhat narrower on account of its smaller cylinders. Introduced by the SECR in 1922, just six were built, for use primarily on the width-restricted Tonbridge to Hastings line. No. 31877 is captured here a mile or so south of Canterbury West, with a long freight from the Isle of Thanet.

24.3.61

The SER kept to level plains and valleys wherever possible, so much so that this bank between Chilham and Chartham is, by SER standards, mountainous. En route to the Isle of Thanet, the long fitted-freight is headed by class N Mogul No. 31848. Station names of the Stour Valley line invite a parody of the train announcement at Ashford: 'Why chill 'em and cart 'em to Canterbury?'.

24.3.61

A pick-up goods on its way to Canterbury West; the menacing bulk of class Q1 0–6–0 No. 33015 is nicely framed between Chilham's signal-box and goods shed, with the tall signal providing a sense of movement and direction. The gear at the end of the platform may have been part of electrification work in progress.

24.3.61

Class Q1 No. 33015, a black beastie, takes water at Canterbury West with the return working of the Ashford pick-up goods. The original station building of 1846 stands beyond the train, a single storey with classical proportions. The platform canopies are more recent; there were originally two over-track sheds alongside the Up and Down buildings.

24.3.61

The bridge over the Great Stour just south of Chilham, with standard class 4 tank No. 80034 heading a stopping train to Ashford. This gentle river rises to the east and west of Ashford and flows northwards through the Downs to meet the North Sea, formerly at Stourmouth (when Thanet was an island) but latterly near Ramsgate at Pegwell Bay.

24.3.61

Class N Mogul No. 31406 heads a train to Margate through a deeply wooded cutting south of Chilham. The leafless overhang of branches brings a sense of chill to this sunny spring scene. Note the narrow waist of the engine, emphasized by the elevated viewpoint and weak shadow.

24.3.61

Bo-Bo class 2 diesel-electric loco No. D5017, with a set of Bulleids near Wye, stands out with almost 3-D effect. The lighting and low camera position also bring out the ballast bin, telegraph pole and the transition from cutting to embankment. The field beyond, epitomizing so many Kentish scenes, could belong to a Roland Hilder painting, while a touch of George Heiron's style is provided by the lone platelayer.

24.3.61

Photographed north of Wye against a backdrop of ash, BR class 4 tank No. 80042 heads a Ramsgate to London Bridge train via Canterbury West and Tonbridge. The cold morning air has condensed a long plume of exhaust steam.

24.3.61

When telegraph poles intrude, a pragmatic solution is to treat them as the centre of composition, splitting but framing this train from Ashford near Wye. The Maunsell set, sandwiched between two SR vans, makes a neat combination, headed by 2–6–4T class 4 No. 80034. BR standard tanks were a 1950s addition to the SECR system, performing well but never looking quite 'at home'.

24.3.61

A class H tank shunts alongside the Rye and Hastings line just east of Ashford. The low bridge, dated 1901, leads to the New Town, built specifically for railway workers, and to the main railway works whose entrance tower can be seen. Opened in 1850 to replace Bricklayer's Arms, Ashford manufactured and repaired engines and rolling stock for the SER/SECR/SR/BR, latterly just for wagons, closing in 1975. There was a large increase in Ashford's railway population in 1911 when the ex-LCDR Longhedge Works closed at Battersea.

15.11.58

The Up 'Golden Arrow' at speed, passing the works and yards at the eastern end of Ashford. This was an opportunist picture, taken from a moving train arriving from Hastings and Rye. The unidentified Pacific gives a great impression of power.

2.6.61

An arrival in the Rye bay at Ashford, with half a former push-pull set at the rear. Waiting passengers on the spacious deck show that raincoats were in vogue during the 1950s, even for sailors. The concrete SR lamp-post resembles a ship's mast with its spars, hangings and top-cable, while the SECR platform canopy has the distinctive shape of an albatross in flight.

15.11.58

Parcels are piled high on Ashford's Down platform, as BR class 4 tank No. 80040 shunts vans. The Maunsell four-wheel utility van on the right was a readily identifiable ambassador of the Southern, wandering all over Britain's railways. Note the single-storey, SER-style station building, also the awnings, dating from around the turn of the century, whose 'straight' pattern was more common to the LCDR.

25.3.61

Cloaked in steam, BR class 4 tank No. 80085 shunts parcels vans beyond the Rye bay at Ashford. Note the complex pointwork below the silhouetted route indicator, especially the trailing three-way point which was characteristic of many ex-SECR junction stations on their Up approaches (see Faversham p. 44 top, Paddock Wood p. 85 bottom and Tonbridge p. 97 top).

25.3.61

Beneath the great signal bridge at the eastern end of Ashford, 'Schools' class V No. 30930 *Radley* arrives with a train from the Hastings and Rye line. Of the forty 'Schools' built, three are preserved: No. 928 *Stowe* on the Bluebell Railway; No. 925 *Cheltenham* in the National Railway Museum; and No. 926 *Repton* on the North Yorkshire Moors Railway.
15.11.58

Four single-track arches at the western end of Ashford match those at Tonbridge as gateways to the Wealden plain. They give the impression of tight clearances for BR class 4 tank No. 80040, departing with assorted vans. The signal gantry looks temporary, possibly necessitated by the impending change to colour-lights.

25.3.61

A fine column of winter steam rises from class L No. 31781 as it restarts from Ashford with a rake of Bulleids, bound for Canterbury and Margate. This was Harry Wainwright's heaviest class of 4–4–0, introduced in 1914 following an easement of weight restrictions. No. 781 was the last of a batch built in Berlin by Borsig, assembled and proven at Ashford by a German work-force, and completed on the opening day of the First World War.

15.11.58

In Ashford's long, open setting, class D1 4–4–0 No. 31489 rests in the Down through platform with a Dover stopping train, while vans are juggled at its rear. In the Up platform, a BR class 4 tank blows off, ready to depart with a Victoria train via Maidstone East.

25.3.61

Ashford's 'other station' was built by the LCDR, the terminus of a long secondary line through Maidstone East from Otford. Opened in 1884, it had a working life of just fifteen years before relegation to goods status following the SECR merger. It was known latterly as Ashford West, a fine memorial to an era of intense competition and reckless investment.

15.11.58

The throat of Ashford West, showing the signal-box, former engine shed and water tower. With a connection to the nearby SER main line, this LCDR presence created a relief route to the Channel ports. It also represented a major step towards the Chatham's ambition to reach Folkestone, thwarted only by virtual bankruptcy and eventual common sense.

15.11.58

# V – Maidstone, Paddock Wood and Hawkhurst

LCDR's Maidstone East is the setting for watering and bunker-trimming BR class 4 tank No. 80087, prior to its crossing the Medway bridge with an Ashford to Victoria train. This was Maidstone's third and most direct route to London, running via Swanley. Electrification reached here in 1939 from the London direction and in 1961 from Ashford.

25.3.61

Just south of Maidstone, an unidentified class H tank heads a rake of BR Mark 1s up the SER's Medway Valley line towards Paddock Wood. Anglers are preparing for a busy day doing nothing on the banks of this placid river. Concrete platelayers' huts were a feature of the SR.

25.3.61

A departure from the staggered platforms of East Farleigh with class H tank No. 31322 and a set of Maunsells en route to Paddock Wood and Tonbridge. This was Maidstone's first railway line, opening in 1844; although double-track and without a terminus, the light passenger trains gave it the character of a branch.

25.3.61

Maunsell push-pull set No. 616 approaches East Farleigh from the west, propelled by class H tank No. 31322. Note the third rail, ready for E-day in June.

25.3.61

Near Teston Crossing, class H tank No. 31517 heads an Up three-coacher of Mark 1s above the river. Having risen near East Grinstead, the Medway cuts through the greensand ridge and the North Downs to join the Thames by Sheerness.

25.3.61

At the same location, class H tank No. 31322 is sandwiched between an SR van and a push-pull set, bound for Maidstone West. Note the platelayers' hut and Second World War pill-box which guarded this stretch of the line.

25.3.61

Steel mineral wagons predominate on this Down freight near Teston Crossing. In contrast to the Stour Valley line, the Type 3 diesels were performing their proper role here on freight duties. The lone figure in the field is apparently lost in contemplation, oblivious of the drumming of the Bo-Bo which shattered the branch line atmosphere.

25.3.61

A fine Kentish landscape near Teston Crossing, seen here with a Down train headed by a Wainwright class H tank. Ripples precluded a clear reflection of trains along this stretch of the Medway.

25.3.61

A country branch train photographed in the Medway Valley near Wateringbury. Class H tank No. 31322 is crystal-clear in the winter sunshine, hauling a push-pull set bound for Paddock Wood and Tonbridge.

25.3.61

A Medway Valley panorama, with class H tank No. 31530 departing Wateringbury with an Up train.

25.3.61

The powerful Tudor architecture of Wateringbury station is the setting for this van train headed by Bo-Bo Type 3 diesel-electric No. D6518, during the transition from steam. Many heavy freight trains on this line ran between Hoo marshalling yard and the Redhill–Guildford line, avoiding the congestion of London.

25.3.61

In essence, 'Thou shalt not cross the line unless thou hast stopped, looked, listened and read the enduring cast-iron notices of the SECR Managing Committee.' Meanwhile, ex-SECR class H tank No. 31517 approaches with a short train of Maunsells, coasting towards Yalding.

25.3.61

At the same location above the Medway, gathering speed with a long trail of steam, a class H tank disappears into the evening of the day with three BR coaches bound for Maidstone West. Such scenes epitomize the harmony of the steam railway with the Kentish countryside.

25.3.61

Carrying no headcode but bound for Maidstone West, class H tank No. 31553 approaches Paddock Wood from Tonbridge along the infinite straightness of the SER's main line. Engineered by William Cubitt, this line was easily graded, no greater than 1 in 264. This compares with 1 in 120 on the Sevenoaks line, 1 in 97 on the Hastings line and 1 in 60 just south of Maidstone West.

22.3.61

Bearing West of England names and double-heading a Down train at Paddock Wood are 'Schools' class V No. 30932 *Blundells* and light Pacific No. 34092 *City of Wells*. Despite the chalked arrow, this is not a boat train but a Bank Holiday through-working. The array of starting signals is a splendid sight.

4.8.59

Fancy pointwork at the eastern end of Paddock Wood where a through train is signalled to infinity. Having shed its pilot, light Pacific No. 34092 *City of Wells* restarts with a gleaming set of Bulleid coaches, about to bear left towards Maidstone West. The old SER signal-box sits astride the start of the Hawkhurst branch which parallels the main line for half a mile. A class C 0–6–0 shunts in the yard to the right.

4.8.59

Ancient and modern, featuring ex-SECR tank No. 31530 and a shiny new set of BR Mark 1s, captured west of Paddock Wood en route to Maidstone West. An early patron and enthusiast of the SER was Charles Dickens who witnessed the transition from stagecoach to railway. In 1865 he was badly shaken in an accident on this line near Staplehurst; although escaping physical injury and helping with the rescue work, he remained in shock until his death five years later, aged fifty-eight.

22.3.61

'West Country' class Pacific No. 34003 *Plymouth* races through Paddock Wood with a train for the Channel ports. Discernible through the engine smoke is the formidable outline of the original station building of 1842: grand, Italianate, substantial, built to last a thousand years, but now sadly demolished.

4.8.59

BR class 4 tank No. 80035 departs Headcorn with a stopping train to Tonbridge, while an unidentified 'Schools' arrives with a Down train. Note the new power signal-box under construction. Beyond, facing Tonbridge, was the former junction with the Kent and East Sussex Railway, one of Colonel Stephens' light railways; it ran via Tenterden to Robertsbridge, part of which is now a preserved steam line.

22.3.61

On the Hawkhurst branch just north of Goudhurst, class H tank No. 31322 brings a Down train across the River Teise, a tributary of the Medway, in a classic country railway scene. Push-pull set No. 732 comprises ex-LSWR corridor stock.

4.8.59

An unusual shot of Goudhurst, featuring boxes for signals, phone calls and letters respectively. The train arriving from Hawkhurst is propelled by class H tank No. 31322. This branch was promoted locally but was taken over by the SER early during construction, opening in 1892–3. The resident engineer was Colonel Holman F. Stephens from Tonbridge, his first line. He went on to build, own and operate a whole empire of little railways nationwide.

4.8.59

The substantial three-storey station house at Cranbrook contrasts with the simple booking office and waiting room alongside. Heading the daily goods is class C 0–6–0 No. 31268 which was built at Ashford in 1904. There were 109 in the class, of which 100 were built at Ashford and nine at Longhedge. No. 592 is preserved on the Bluebell Railway in SECR Brunswick green and with a polished brass dome.

4.8.59

Built on a curve in the High Weald, Cranbrook station had a grand setting. Class H tank No. 31266 coasts its train into the single platform, bound for Paddock Wood. Although picturesque, the station was inconveniently sited, over a mile from the town that it served.

4.8.59

An end-view of Cranbrook station, with class C 0–6–0 No. 31268 about to exchange wagons in the yard. Like other early classes of the SECR, it was built under the direction of Harry Wainwright, but with detailed design by his chief draughtsman, Robert Surtees, a gifted locomotive engineer from the LCDR.

4.8.59

Tenders for class C were exceptionally long, as seen here in a beechwood cutting south of Cranbrook. No. 31268 is running tender-first with the pick-up goods, neither crewman watching the road ahead. Together with its class H contemporary shown opposite, they provide a suitable tribute to Harry Wainwright, the SECR's superintendent of locomotives and rolling stock until his retirement in 1913. He had previously succeeded his father as Carriage and Wagon Superintendent of the South Eastern.

4.8.59

The first train of the day arrives in light mist at Hawkhurst, in the care of class H tank No. 31266. The two-road engine shed beyond is closed, a relic of busier pre-war days. Both passenger and goods traffic were in terminal decline, with the bay and sidings to the right overgrown and virtually disused. Agricultural and hop-pickers' traffic had been its life-blood; the last hoppers' special ran in 1959 and the line closed in 1961.

4.8.59

The Hawkhurst branch was 11½ miles long and climbed a series of 1 in 60 and 1 in 80 banks to the summit at Badgers Oak tunnel. This was midway between Cranbrook and Hawkhurst, on the watershed of the High Weald. Class H tank No. 31266 emerges with a Down train into rich woodlands at the south portal. The shed plate is 74D for Tonbridge.

4.8.59

Departure of the first train of the day from Hawkhurst, propelled by class H tank No. 31266. This view from the top of the water tower shows the station throat on a curve, a configuration frequently used by railway modellers. The layout at Hawkhurst was suitable for possible extension southwards; although a South Kent Railway was proposed in 1895, the SER was unimpressed and killed it.

4.8.59

A young enthusiast at Hawkhurst, terminus of the branch, with class H tank No. 31266 and push-pull set. The pristine lad is apparently torn between his mother's commands and his desire to join the fireman on the engine. Like Dunton Green, the underside of the canopy is boarded; like Cranbrook, the station was a mile or so from the town; like warm summers from the 1930s, the Hawkhurst branch is remembered as a model of perfection.

4.8.59

# VI – Ore to Tonbridge and Sevenoaks

BR class 4 tank No. 80041 emerges from Ore tunnel with a Hastings to Ashford train via Rye. This line was opened in 1851 to create a strategic link along the south coast in the interests of national security. The electric train shed beyond was used by Brighton and Victoria stock which terminated at Ore.

6.5.61

Deep in the Ore Valley between tunnels, a BR standard class 4 tank heads a train to Rye and Ashford, a line shortly to be dieselized. A further tribute to steam is the old power station on the hillside, replaced during the 1960s by a new gas turbine plant.

6.5.61

Mountfield tunnel, one of four on the Tonbridge to Hastings line which were built with less than the specified number of linings. Extra courses were subsequently added, resulting in narrow tunnels. For 135 years, Restriction 0 (8 ft) stock served this line until the offending tunnels were singled and electrified in 1986. A narrow DMU, all-stations to Tunbridge Wells, is seen here at the north portal in 1964.

Bo-Bo type 3 diesels were introduced by the Southern Region in 1960. Built by the Birmingham Railway Carriage & Wagon Co. to BR design, they had Sulzer engines and Crompton generators. As a final gesture to the civil contractor who swindled the SER, a batch of twelve was built with narrow bodies for the Hastings line. This is D6587, resting at Hastings with a mixed freight. Such traffic would soon become extinct on most of the Southern.

8.7.63

A scene which once typified the Hastings line until the DMUs took over in 1958: a 4–4–0 express engine heading a set of narrow-bodied Maunsell stock. Class D1 No. 31735 hauls its train between High Brooms and Tonbridge, having originated on the LBSCR system.

20.3.60

Just south of Tonbridge is the south portal of Somerhill tunnel, which was singled in 1986 to accommodate full-width (9 ft) EMUs. Previously, the line to Tunbridge Wells could accommodate only Restriction 1 stock (8 ft 6 in). Running light to Tonbridge is an unidentified class U1 Mogul. The white substance on the bank is a mystery, although it looks like lime.

20.3.60

Amid thickets of silver birch, class N Mogul No. 31851 climbs from Tonbridge to High Brooms with a train for Eridge and Brighton. The coldness of the scene truly reflects the bleakness of the day, but produced spectacular exhaust effects in both sight and sound.

20.3.60

East of Tonbridge on the SER main line, a parabolic overbridge frames a Down train headed by class N Mogul No. 31406. In his essay *The Flight*, Charles Dickens describes the 'dreamy pleasure' of travel on this line 'among the harvest and the Kentish hops'. With remarkable foresight, he eagerly anticipated air travel to Paris, but made no mention of a Channel tunnel.

22.3.61

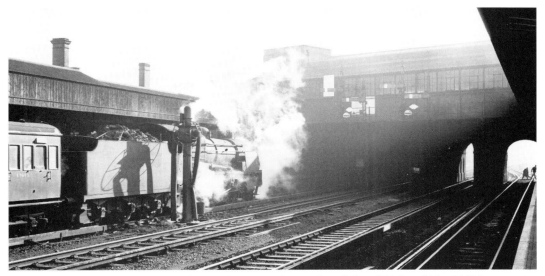

Grotesque shadows of a water column play upon the tender of class N Mogul No. 31826, at rest in the Down platform at Tonbridge. The booking office looms above four single-track arches, forming a symbolic gateway to Wealden Kent – only the portcullises are missing! The Hastings line comes in from the right where two railwaymen are crossing the Up tracks.

22.3.61

Great billows of steam and heavily clad ramblers are evidence of a cold, crisp but sunny morning at Tonbridge. An unidentified class C 0–6–0 transfers a parcels van from the bay to a train in the Down through platform. The central tracks lead directly to the Sevenoaks line which curves to the right of the signal-box.

22.3.61

Between Redhill and Ashford, the SER main line is gently graded and almost dead straight; where bluffs were encountered, the line went through rather than round. In this sandy cutting east of Tonbridge, a tall overbridge frames the rebuilt 'West Country' class Pacific No. 34016 *Bodmin*, heading a train for the Channel ports.

22.3.61

Tonbridge was a great hub of the SER, with lines converging from four directions and with services arriving from six or seven. There is steam-a-plenty here as class N Mogul No. 31826 restarts from the Down platform to pass beneath the great bridge carrying the A21 and the main buildings. In *The Flight*, Dickens describes a five-minute stop here for refreshments, during his journey from London Bridge to Paris via Folkestone.

22.3.61

Intricately trussed, gracefully arched and cantilevered, this SR signal-bridge spans the three Up lines at Tonbridge. 'West Country' class Pacific No. 34037 *Clovelly* is waiting for the off; from the forest of semaphores, the fourth from the left is about to rise, the train bound for Charing Cross via Redhill.

20.3.60

Class U1 Mogul No. 31909 restarts from Tonbridge's Up loop with a train for the old main line to Redhill; the locomotive, coaches, signals, track layout, even the yard lamp, all date from the inter-war period of the Southern Railway, probably 1935 when the west end of Tonbridge was realigned to ease the curve to Sevenoaks.

20.3.60

Up starting signalry at Tonbridge provides a strong frame for BR class 4 tank No. 80147 as it crosses all main lines to bring a train of Maunsells into the Down main platform. The ball factory is a reminder that cricket originated in this neck of the woods.

20.3.60

Opened in 1868, the cut-off via Sevenoaks to Tonbridge reduced the SER's route distance by 13 miles compared with the Redhill dog-leg. Although difficult and expensive to build, it was deemed necessary in order to compete with the LCDR's more direct route to Dover. Here at the 26-mile marker, class N Mogul No. 31404 heads an Up mixed-goods train. A few sheep safely graze alongside Hildenborough's distant signal.

7.6.60

The Up 'Golden Arrow' approaches Weald Intermediate signal-box. Evening sunshine reflects from the straight-sided Pullman coaches and from the clean, dark green cladding of light Pacific No. 34086 *219 Squadron*. The engine commemorates the Blenheim coastal-patrol fighters based at Catterick, with two victories during the Battle of Britain. This train's Paris to London journey time of 7½ hours compares with some 11 hours in the mid-nineteenth century and 3 hours by Eurostar.

7.6.60

Grass and wild flowers are in abundance around Weald Intermediate signal-box, as 'Battle of Britain' class Pacific No. 34078 *222 Squadron* flies past with a train to Charing Cross. It commemorates the Spitfires from Kirton-le-Lindsay, Lincs., with forty-nine victories.

7.6.60

Chugging up the four miles of Hildenborough bank, class H tank No. 31278 approaches Weald Intermediate with a rake of Maunsells bound for Sevenoaks.

7.6.60

North of Weald Intermediate, 'West Country' class No. 34027 *Taw Valley* passes the 25-mile marker at speed, with a Down express for the Channel ports. The 'stone hills' loom beyond, a ridge of greensand which necessitated a two-mile tunnel and this long, 1 in 122 approach. Like many classes of engine, the rebuilt Pacifics lost much of their good looks when grubby.

7.6.60

On the down grade out of Sevenoaks tunnel 'West Country' class Pacific No. 34004 *Yeovil* enters the Wealden plain with the 'The Man of Kent'. Although the locomotive carries no headboard, the name is displayed above the windows of the Mark 1 coaches.

7.6.60

A Hastings DMU emerges from Sevenoaks tunnel into this grand cutting to pass light Pacific No. 34070 *Manston* with an Up train to Victoria. The engine commemorates the Thanet aerodrome which was a front line daytime base used by fighters during the Battle of Britain.

7.6.60

Viewed from above the south portal, an unidentified class H tank propels its push-pull set towards Sevenoaks tunnel. The cutting (through Wealden clay) is wide and modestly angled to avoid landslips; it draws one's eye neatly into the rich countryside of the 'Garden of England' and to the distant ridge of the High Weald.

7.6.60

'West Country' class Pacific No. 34012 *Launceston* emerges from Sevenoaks tunnel with a train for the Channel ports. The clutter on the right is evidence of work in progress at weekends and nights for impending electrification and colour-light signalling.

7.6.60

At the north portal of Sevenoaks tunnel there is further evidence of electrification work, with the third rail resting on the Down track, awaiting installation. Class H tank No. 31177 propels a push-pull set into the smoky abyss, amid the ferns and dense undergrowth at this dank, shady end of the tunnel.

7.6.60

Sevenoaks had a magnificent set of Southern Railway semaphores, with all four roads signalled in the Up direction for the SER and LCDR lines. Nosing into the scene is light Pacific No. 34088 *213 Squadron*. Note the barley-sugar lamp-posts with an odd mix of gas lamps – SR on the left, earlier on the right. Did the Second World War perhaps interrupt their renewal?

7.6.60

This parcels train at Sevenoaks is about to bear left up the main line to Orpington, headed by class N Mogul No. 31855. Tubs Hill has been painted out of the platform name-board, a sub-title formerly used to distinguish this from the LCDR's Bat and Ball station nearby. All lines from London to Sevenoaks were electrified in 1935, but it was not until 1961 that SER electrification was completed to Dover.

7.6.60

In the steeply cut, densely wooded northern approach to Sevenoaks tunnel, 'West Country' class Pacific No. 34091 *Weymouth* heads a train for the Channel ports. Note the unique colour-light signal which shone into the tunnel from the Up side, installed by the SR to improve visibility and safety within.

7.6.60

Although they performed well, BR standard class 5s never looked 'at home' in the south-east; their more natural habitat was surely the industrial Midlands and the north? Passing through Sevenoaks with a Continental express of Bulleid stock is No. 73084. The driving wheels look much larger than those of the Bulleid Pacifics (see next picture), but this is an illusion; they were both 6 ft 2 in diameter.

13.9.59

'West Country' class Pacific No. 34103 *Calstock* looks quite 'at home' as it races through Sevenoaks with yet another train-load of Continental travellers. The bridge apertures seem scarcely big enough for such giants of steam.

13.9.59

Any old iron? A spell of construction duty at Sevenoaks for class H tank No. 31505, with trucks and materials for use in tunnel electrification work. According to the poster, there's no better life than as a policeman – unless, of course, one can drive a Wainwright tank engine! That is now a rare privilege, since only a few have been preserved (four Ps and an H).

7.6.60

# VII – Redhill to Dorking and Chilworth

Class N Mogul No. 31869 enters Redhill with a train from Reading and Guildford. Note the ornate SER valancing to the platform canopy; there were many variations to this design (for example see London Bridge low-level p. 146 top).

17.8.58

Redhill is the junction for Tonbridge, Brighton and Guildford. On the island platform, the number of Down starting signals was minimized by the use of SR mechanical route indicators. The result was this neat array of two, neatly arranged on rail-built posts, together with shunting discs and track-circuit diamonds. They frame an unidentified class N Mogul as it backs into platform 1.

17.8.58

It was usual in summer for at least one ex-Great Western engine to make a daily round-trip from Reading to Redhill. Here, 4–6–0 No. 7813 *Freshford Manor* heads a return working on the 2-mile straight to the west of Reigate. The Birkenhead through-service would reverse at Redhill, with sections for Sussex (Brighton–Eastbourne–Hastings) and for Kent (Canterbury West–Margate and Dover–Sandwich).

7.6.63

At the same location Maunsell class N No. 31627 heads an Up train, its wheels seemingly brushing the grasses. Trains on this line provide a suitable tribute to R.E.L. Maunsell who became Chief Mechanical Engineer of the SECR in 1913, recruited from the Great Southern and Western Railway of Ireland. His qualities of sound engineering, hard work and leadership were such that many key staff followed him in 1923 to the SR where he remained CME until retirement in 1937, aged sixty-nine.

7.6.63

111

Class U Mogul No. 31615 heads an Up train of flat-sided ex-Hastings stock, near the end of the long straight to the west of Reigate. In deference to Richard Maunsell and his Irish connection, an apt title for this cross-country line would be the 'Great Southern and Western'. Class U was introduced by Maunsell in 1928, a development of his two-cylinder class K tank, itself a derivative of the ubiquitous N.

7.6.63

A Down train pollutes the Wealden plain near Reigate, a reminder of the dirtiness as well as the romance of steam. The line's preponderance of Maunsell coaching stock during the 'swinging sixties' is a further tribute to this revered mogul of an engineer.

7.6.63

At the same location an unidentified BR class 4 Mogul stokes its fire. Despite evidence of the leading box van, this was a passenger service bound for Reading. Note the huge quarries in the North Downs escarpment, site of the former Dorking Greystone Lime Company.

7.6.63

A crossing-keeper's cottage beneath a resplendent ash, with class N Mogul No. 31852 heading an Up train of mixed BR and Bulleid stock. The signals belong to Betchworth station, just around the curve to the left. Note the open porch with a genuine birdcage, indicative of the warmth of this delightful June day.

7.6.63

A crew-member watches the road ahead into Betchworth where a 20 m.p.h. speed restriction is in force. The train is headed by class N Mogul No. 31819. Such scenes evoke fond memories of the sights, sounds and atmosphere of the steam railway in the south-east. Note the contrast of undergrowth and grasses between the north and south faces of the cutting.

7.6.63

Following the dieselization of services to Tunbridge Wells West, BR standard 2–6–4 tanks were transferred to help work the Guildford line. Here, an unidentified class 4 restarts a short Up train from Betchworth. Note the cottage-style building on the Down side: tall, ornate and partially tile-hung.

7.6.63

Class N Mogul No. 31863 heads an Up train between Deepdene and Betchworth. This line was an early extension to the SER, opening in 1849. Its primary role was strategic, to provide direct connection between the GWR/LSWR and the Channel ports, avoiding London. It was dieselized in 1964, and nowadays carries the Reading–Gatwick Airport service.

7.6.63

The Southern was a pioneer in the use of concrete, including the occasional signal post. This is Betchworth's Up distant signal, providing a suitable setting for class U Mogul No. 31622 heading a Down train. Note the rich undergrowth, forever trying to re-establish the primeval forest of the Weald.

7.6.63

In a lively display of motion, a long through-freight approaches Betchworth from the east, headed by class N Mogul No. 31411. Although generally accredited to Maunsell, the design of class N was influenced by Harry Holcroft and G.H. Pears who were recruited from the GWR. Less handsome than its GWR counterparts, the N had design similarities with class 43xx which was introduced in 1911, six years ahead of the N.

7.6.63

Class Q1 No. 33034 fulfils its primary role of freight haulage, on a long train of four-wheelers and bogie vans en route to Guildford. The location is a mile and a half east of Deepdene beneath a light bridge which carries a track to Wentworth Hall on the Downs.

7.6.63

Below Box Hill, ex-GWR 4–6–0 No. 7813 *Freshford Manor* heads an Up train east of Deepdene. As in the previous picture, wild flowers are in abundance.

7.6.63

Just east of Deepdene, class U Mogul No. 31622 crosses the LBSCR's Leatherhead–Horsham line with a train to Redhill. There used to be a spur here to the Brighton line, operational from 1867–1900 and from 1941–7. Although the LBSCR reached Dorking eighteen years after the SECR, it provided a more direct route to London and was electrified in 1929. The SECR line was electrified in 1932 only between Redhill and Reigate.

7.6.63

A departure to Redhill, having set down two Girl Guides and a Boy Scout. They may have been bound for the open spaces of Box Hill, the original name of this station until it changed in 1923 to Deepdene. The gent on the right, with sack and bicycle, looks like the postman.

26.5.63

The cab and nearside cylinder of class N Mogul No. 31821 as it draws into Deepdene with an afternoon train from Guildford. The light construction, timber-clad, single-storey building is typically SER but unique on this line.

26.5.63

Two features of the Redhill–Guildford line were its long straight stretches and the use of redundant stock from other lines. Both characteristics are brought out here on the Dorking bank, with the evening sun reflected from the flat-sided ex-Hastings coaches bound for Guildford.

26.5.63

Class U Mogul No. 31627 leads both its Up train and one's eyes to the staggered platforms of Dorking Town station. The tall SR signal is set against a scattering of cotton-wool cloud.

31.7.60

Exhaust steam blends with cumulus as class N Mogul No. 31863 departs Dorking Town with a train for Guildford. Note the ornate eaves of the cottage-style station building.

31.7.60

Class N Mogul No. 31852 on the long approach to Dorking Town with a freight bound for Redhill.
26.5.63

In a rural setting below the Pilgrim's Way on the North Downs, class N Mogul No. 31851 heads a pilgrimage of Maunsell stock out of Dorking, bound for Guildford. Only one of this once-ubiquitous class has been preserved, No. 874 on the Mid-Hants Railway.

31.7.60

Warm evening sunlight illuminates this Up train near Gomshall, comprising eight coaches and class U Mogul No. 31623. Of the fifty engines built, two of class U are preserved on the Bluebell Railway and two more on the Mid-Hants Railway.

31.7.60

An Up goods train negotiates the staggered platforms of Gomshall and Shere, headed by class Q1 0–6–0 No. 33022. The strong frontal sun brings out the cloud as well as the telegraph pole, signals, gas lamp, Bulleid's horseshoe of a smokebox, and the cluster of trolleys on the platform.

22.6.63

Ex-Great Western 4–6–0 No. 7824 *Iford Manor* departs Gomshall with a train for Reading, framed by a pair of tall SR lattice-post signals. Since only the Southern used destination discs and with six positions, this visitor lacks a full set of pegs but sports a couple of lamps on the buffer beam and a white rectangle at the top.

22.6.63

This Up train near Gomshall is headed by class N Mogul No. 31851. The side-lighting is put to good effect to create a classic scene of a steam train in the countryside.

22.6.63

The same cutting from the opposite direction, with class N Mogul No. 31870 on a Down train. This different viewpoint portrays a more open landscape, but it lacks the vivid shadow and texture of the previous picture.

22.6.63

An open Wealden landscape on Albury Heath, between Gomshall and Chilworth, featuring class N Mogul No. 31868 on a Down train, with a jumble of old sleepers.

22.6.63

An Up train to the east of Chilworth, headed by class N Mogul No. 31865. The line here is on the fringe of the greensand, a mile from the Downs, an enforced deviation to avoid despoiling the Tudor manor house and estates of Albury Park.

22.6.63

A long freight tackles the bank through Albury Heath, headed by an unidentified class N. The Up track had recently been relaid with flat-bottom rail, hence the discarded sleepers on the right. The Down track is still bullhead.

22.6.63

A Down train coasts towards Chilworth, headed by class N Mogul No. 31611. After deviating around Albury Park, the line reasserts itself here, sheltered below the scarp of the North Downs.

22.6.63

As dusk descends, class N Mogul No. 31864 departs Chilworth & Albury with a Down train of vans and coaches. The fireman is not brandishing a section token, but a coaling iron.

22.6.63

# VIII – The Westerham Branch to Charing Cross

Between the water tower and the signal-box, class H tank No. 31543 enters Westerham with an ancient push-pull set. The signalman rests on the steps; with one engine in steam, there were no tokens to exchange. The branch was just 4½ miles long, and its proximity to the metropolis made it a favourite haunt for steam enthusiasts.

22.4.59

Westerham's setting is open and rural when viewed from this quarter. Class H No. 31520 stands in the platform road; the goods shed is to the left and a railwayman gazes wistfully towards an inn to the right.

13.9.59

The run-round loop at Westerham, with class H tank No. 31520 gently simmering in the platform with a push-pull set. The weather-boarded, single-storey building has a family resemblance with other SER branch stations such as Cliffe and Sharnal Street, but the awning is special to the independently promoted Westerham Valley Railway which opened in 1881.

13.9.59

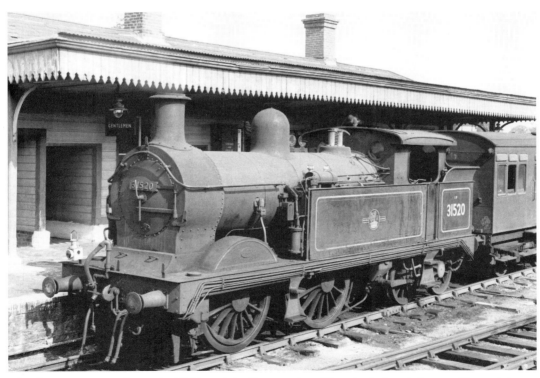

The distinctive pagoda roof of Wainwright-Surtees class H tanks imbued them with quaintness rather than elegance. Built between 1904 and 1915 for London suburban duty, No. 31520 is seen here in the autumn of its days, resting at Westerham. Of the original sixty-six engines, only No. 263 has survived, restored in Brunswick green on the Bluebell Railway.

13.9.59

Push-pull set No. 482 between Westerham and Brasted, powered by class H tank No. 31520. The set comprises the coach portions of two former SECR steam motorsets.

13.9.59

On the branch's last day of operation, class H tank No. 31263 departs Brasted for Westerham. The long station building was built with a full set of offices and facilities which were scarcely warranted by traffic receipts.

29.10.61

On a warm afternoon class H tank No. 31520 operates near Brasted with a Down train. Sadly the Westerham branch was closed in 1961. Construction of the M25 motorway engulfed the old railway for a couple of miles, thereby killing aspirations to reopen it as a private venture. Not one SECR line is preserved for steam.

13.9.59

Although relegated to a halt during its latter years, Brasted retained its architectural dignity in this quiet, rural setting. Push-pull set No. 482 approaches from the Westerham direction, propelled by class H tank No. 31520. The station name was formerly displayed in whitened stones upon the bank to the right.

13.9.59

A classic country railway scene showing Brasted and its modest goods yard, with push-pull set No. 610 departing for Dunton Green propelled by a class H tank. This set of SR Maunsells had displaced the old SECR stock.

14.5.61

The intimacy of the country branch is brought out in this photograph of class H tank No. 31551 on a Down train, approaching Brasted out of a shallow cutting.

11.3.61

For reasons unknown a long mixed-freight, bound for the Channel ports, took refuge on the initial curve of the Westerham branch, headed by class N Mogul No. 31828. Dunton Green's station buildings are visible in the background. Note the home signal which was leaning some five degrees out of true.

22.4.59

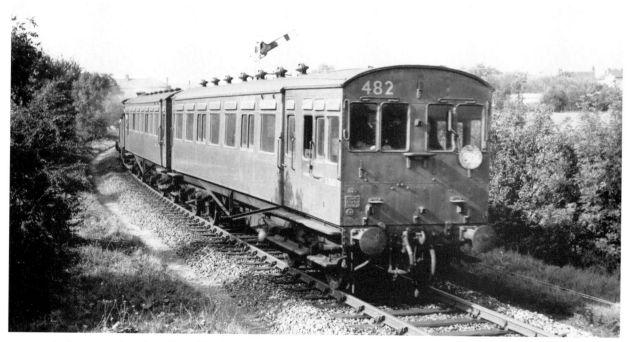

A close-up of push-pull set No. 482 approaching Dunton Green. Each coach was originally integral with a stubby-looking 0–4–0 tank engine, eight of which were introduced by the SECR in 1904–5 for branch line duties. They were converted into more conventional push-pull sets prior to the First World War, and survived remarkably well.

13.9.59

Inside the parlour of ex-SECR set No. 482, with its well finished woodwork and kingsize end-seats. Note the window-straps on the benches and the fire extinguisher by the door. The lone traveller is the author's younger sister.

13.9.59

Dunton Green's station buildings were in the V between the branch and the Up main line. Class H tank No. 31177 and its driver pose at the end of the connecting tunnel; as the poster says, 'May time is camera time'.

15.5.61

Crystal-clear and making some impressive smoke, a Down parcels is headed by 'Schools' class V No. 30922 *Marlborough* north of Dunton Green. 'Schools' were once commonplace here before DMUs took over the Hastings services in 1958. During the war *Marlborough* was shot up by the Luftwaffe around Westenhanger.

22.4.59

The front detail of class H tank No. 31518 in the bay at Dunton Green. Although working out of Tonbridge, the shed-plate still shows 73D for Gillingham, a reminder of steam's heyday in North Kent. The boarded underside of the canopy brings a touch of Victorian splendour to this fine station.

13.9.59

Near Dunton Green, 'Battle of Britain' class Pacific No. 34073 *249 Squadron* emerges from the bushes with an Up boat train. This engine commemorates the Hurricanes from Church Fenton, Yorks., with seventy-five victories.

22.4.59

A farewell to steam on the Westerham branch, with class H tank No. 31263. This silhouette could represent so many Southern branches, leaving an impression of sedate travel in charming little trains from the golden age of country railways.

29.10.61

A humble duty for 'Schools' class V No. 30927 *Clifton*, approaching Polhill tunnel with a short parcels train bound for London Bridge low-level or Bricklayer's Arms. In 1941 *Clifton* was damaged in a bombing raid at Nine Elms shed.

7.6.60

Coal-smoke pollutes Kentish orchards half a mile north of Dunton Green, as an unidentified class BB Pacific heads an eleven-coach train of Bulleid stock bound for the Channel ports. This is the Darent Valley which cuts through the North Downs to the right.

28.5.60

Light Pacific No. 34070 *Manston* ploughs between the fields on the down grade south of Polhill tunnel, with a train for the Channel ports. There are Pullman coaches towards the rear, which were regularly incorporated into boat trains.

7.6.60

The 'Golden Arrow' insignia obscures the identity of a 'BB' class Pacific as it battles its way up the 1 in 143 gradient between Dunton Green and Polhill tunnel, serving as a final commemoration to the Battle of Britain.

28.5.60

Not as grand as northern hills but quietly beautiful, the North Downs provided some rich settings for the steam railway. Here a 'Battle of Britain' class Pacific banks towards the south entrance to Polhill tunnel, another major piece of engineering, a mile and a half long. The semi-legible number on the cab looks like 340x2.

7.6.60

The SER main line was quadrupled as far as Orpington by 1905. A Down boat train approaches between Orpington's extensive EMU sidings and sheds, headed by 'Merchant Navy' class No. 35001 *Channel Packet*. Just three heavy Pacifics were allocated to Stewarts Lane at this time (see Dover p. 61 for *Rotterdam Lloyd* and p. 59 bottom for *Clan Line*).

22.4.59

Class D1 4–4–0 No. 31739 stands with parcels vans in London Bridge low-level, awaiting departure to Redhill. This was the site of London's first passenger terminus, opened in 1836 by the London and Greenwich Railway (absorbed into the SER in 1845). It crossed the marshes of Bermondsey and Deptford on a brick viaduct. As SER and LBSCR traffic grew, London Bridge expanded to twenty-two tracks with an eleven-track approach, but the low-level retained the aura of a quiet, historic backwater.
15.9.58

'West Country' class Pacific No. 34021 *Dartmoor* trundles through platform 3 at London Bridge, with a mid-morning train to the Channel ports. The station looks as desolate as Dartmoor itself, in contrast to the congestion and uncertainties of twice-daily rush-hours. The SER's costly West End extension opened in 1864 to compete with the LCDR's new lines to Victoria and the City. It was packed with interesting junctions.

25.5.60

The last days of steam also saw the end of semaphore signalling on SECR main lines. A colour-light gantry is under construction at the country end of Grove Park, and this neat trio of stubby starting signals will soon disappear. They were a through-line alternative to SR mechanical route indicators (for example see Ashford p. 74 and Redhill p. 110 top). To the right, a Hastings DMU is crossing the Bromley North branch.

11.3.61

Forty-five years after his retirement Harry Wainwright lends a hand on a hazy morning at Cannon Street, as class C No. 31317 gently manoeuvres an EMU driving-coach which had suffered collision damage. The platforms here extend half-way across the Thames. Cannon Street was the SER's City terminus, also hosting trains from the LBSCR, LSWR and LNWR during its early years.

August 1958

The final half-mile into Charing Cross is lined by a varied assortment of rooftops. Running tender-first, 'West Country' class Pacific No. 34005 *Barnstaple* hauls empty stock past the Shell building (under construction). The picture is taken from the former junction platform at Waterloo where a single track ran through the old LSWR station. This connection was severed in 1911 during rebuilding of the LSWR terminal.

30.8.59